Beautiful Feet

A 30-Day Devotional Journey

By Deb Burma

CONCORDIA PUBLISHING HOUSE · SAINT LOUIS

Begin your daily devotion time in prayer.

Heavenly Father,
Thank You for giving me beautiful feet!
I praise You for the gifts of forgiveness and salvation
in Christ, as You have proclaimed them to me
in Your Word.
As I receive hope and encouragement from this
devotion today, fill me with Your Holy Spirit that I may
learn and grow in faith as I walk in Your Word.
In Jesus' precious name I pray. Amen.

4 5 6 7 8 9 10 11 12 13   26 25 24 23 22 21 20 19 18 17

Introduction

Take a look at your gorgeous tootsies right now. Perhaps you look down at perfectly polished toes and attractive arches; maybe you are faced, instead, with crooked toes and calluses, blisters and bunions. Regardless of their outward appearance, your feet are declared beautiful by God! He has equipped you with uniquely beautiful feet for your walk with Him.

Your feet take you many places in your daily walk. Right now, maybe they are aching to be put up. Perhaps your feet are so busy running in all directions that rest is rare. Set aside some time each day to rest those tired tootsies. Open this book, and take a closer look at your feet and the feet of others, too, as you learn of God's grace in Christ, who walks alongside you and forgives your sins. (Now that's some toe-tapping good news!) Learn what makes truly beautiful feet and what the Lord calls those feet to do. Prepare to be swept off your feet by your Savior as you walk in His Word; kick up your heels with joy in the Lord because He has declared your feet beautiful!

"How beautiful are the feet of those who bring good news!" (Romans 10:15 NIV).

I pray that these devotions will put a spring in your step, fill you with hope and encouragement, and support you in your daily walk with Christ. As the Lord speaks to you in His Word, the Holy Spirit will guide you and empower you as you walk with Him. I can't wait for you to jump in with both feet!

Serving Christ,

Deb Burma, author

A Map for Your Path

> And your ears shall hear a word behind you, say-
> ing, "This is the way, walk in it," when you turn to
> the right or when you turn to the left. Isaiah 30:21

Maps are fascinating pieces of work, especially those created for walking trails and hiking paths through the wilderness and over rough terrain. When accurately drawn and precisely to scale, a map will show every twist and turn on the trail; it will point out elevation changes and every landmark along the way. With this kind of map in our hands, we can navigate our way through the most difficult parts of a trail, as long as we are careful to check the map regularly to make sure that we stay on course.

How is your daily walk with God? Have you checked God's "map" lately to make sure you are on His path and not aimlessly wandering? Or have you proudly thought you could brave your journey alone and without need of direction? God's map, of course, is His Word. As He speaks to us in the Bible, He says, "This is the way, walk in it." All the directions we need for our journey through this life are found in our map, the Bible. With complete accuracy and precision, God's Word shows us how to navigate through every twist and turn in our lives and gives us strength by the power of the Holy Spirit to get through the roughest portions of our journey.

Without a map for our path, we would wander off course and become completely lost. Although we wander away in our sin, our Mapmaker and Guide finds us and forgives us in Christ, setting our feet back on the trail. He guides us down the one true path to heaven—Jesus Christ, our Savior. He gives us clear direction and purpose, walks beside us every step of the way, and fills our hearts with faith through the Holy Spirit.

For real direction on life's journey, your beautiful feet need to be walking in the Word! Pray that the Spirit will put a passion in your heart for God's Word. Keep digging into it. In addition to weekly worship, try a daily Bible reading plan or a devotion book (like this one) that guides your journey into the Scriptures with topics relevant to you. Choose verses and memorize them; God uses His Word, hidden in your heart, to guide and encourage you just when you need it. If it seems overwhelming to add something else to your day, remember that God doesn't seek to make our paths more complicated. On the contrary, He helps us recognize and remove the unnecessary things on our path as we seek His will first, reading our map and letting Him speak to us and navigate us in His Word. Remember that God's Word never returns void; it always accomplishes the purposes for which He sent it (Isaiah 55:11).

Dear God, Thank You for Your map, which provides me with all the directions I need for my journey with Jesus at my side. Fill me with Your Spirit that I may delight in Your directions, read them every day, and stay on course. In Jesus' name. Amen.

A Real Boost

He drew me up from the pit of destruction,
out of the miry bog, and set my feet upon a rock,
making my steps secure. Psalm 40:2

Are your beautiful feet looking for a real boost? a big pick-me-up? a total lift? Do you want to walk tall? Look no further: platform shoes are your answer! Unlike a high heel that lifts only the back half of your foot and bends the other half into strange and painful contortions, a platform shoe boosts your entire foot, and suddenly, you are walking five inches taller than before! This outrageously funny shoe gives us a real boost, reminding us of our walk with the Lord.

Here's the *real* boost. When you are feeling about two inches tall, insignificant and low, when you are thinking, "Who am I that anyone should care? Who am I that the Lord would listen to my prayers?"—know this: your Creator reaches down to you where you are and lovingly draws you up. He who stretched the heavens and formed the earth is crazy about little old you! He knows everything about you; He even knows and cares about what you are doing and thinking right now. The psalmist proclaims: "You know when I sit down and when I rise up; You discern my thoughts from afar" (Psalm 139:2).

Maybe at this moment you are feeling unforgivable because you just keep falling into that same old sin over and over. Or maybe you are convinced that your sins are too great and too numerous to deserve forgiveness. Satan will attempt to trip you up and stomp all over you with his lies. He wants you to think you're not forgivable. But God says you are! Your soul needs relining with the cushioning comfort of God's forgiveness and grace, which are yours in Christ Jesus, as proclaimed in His Word.

Receive this *real* boost: Our heavenly Father lavishes His grace on you, redeeming you from your sins (Ephesians 1:7-8). His love for you is so great, He sent His Son to die for you in the midst of your sin (Romans 5:8). You have been chosen by God, saved by grace through faith, adopted as His own child (Ephesians 1:4-5; 2:8). You are God's workmanship (Ephesians 2:10). He created you and lovingly formed you, knitting you together in your mother's womb (Psalm 139:13). He has called you by name and you belong to Him (Isaiah 43:1). He has a special plan for you (Jeremiah 29:11), and He will never leave you nor forsake you (Hebrews 13:5-6). Nothing can happen to you apart from His will (Matthew 10:29-31).

God's Word speaks to us and fills us with a love that is so perfect and unconditional that no matter how low or small, imperfect or unforgivable we may feel, He is able to boost us up in His grace and love—to lift us in a way that no platform shoe could ever do! He sets our feet upon the rock of Christ, making our steps secure. That is the ultimate boost!

*Lord, Your Word proclaims the limitless love and grace
You lavish upon me in Christ, giving me the real boost
I need for my weary soul. Thank You for setting my feet
upon the rock of Jesus Christ, my firm foundation.
In His name. Amen.*

Beautiful Feet

> How beautiful are the feet of those
> who bring good news! Romans 10:15 (NIV)

Nothing beats a well-laced, arch-supporting, great-fitting pair of athletic shoes for a good walk or run; this is where the rubber meets the road, literally! Nothing is more comfortable or better for our feet in the "long run." And these shoes can remind us of a very important part of our walk in this life. They give us truly beautiful feet because of what they signify.

In Romans 10:15, the apostle Paul quotes the words of Isaiah, who spoke of the good news sent by messengers, running to declare Israel's release from captivity in Babylon. (Check out Isaiah 52!) Paul uses the same words to describe the messengers sent to declare the ultimate Good News: our release from captivity to sin.

You have been sent to run with the Good News to a world in need of a Savior! "Gospel" means, literally, "Good News." The Gospel of our Lord and Savior, Jesus Christ, is that His death and resurrection paid for our sins. It promises us eternity in heaven by faith. This is the Good News; this is the cornerstone of our faith. This is the message with which we are sent!

Clad in your athletic shoes, you are the messenger! The message of Good News in Romans was so beautiful that its beauty was transferred to the messenger, declaring his feet "beautiful" (no matter how they really looked)! Now, with the Gospel message in your hands and athletic shoes on your beautiful feet, you are the messenger!

You may be thinking, "I don't know if I have what it takes to be a messenger. It's such a scary and overwhelming task. I don't know where to begin!" Maybe you are even thinking, "If this is the task of my beautiful feet, then I'm giving my sneakers to the thrift store!" When was the last time you told an unbeliever about Jesus? Has it been a long time? never?

Never fear! You can share the Good News in your walk (or run), empowered by the Holy Spirit. Begin by praying for people in your life who do not appear to have faith. Ask the Holy Spirit to work faith in their hearts, and pray that God would give you an opportunity to talk about Jesus with them. Establish relationships with nonbelievers at work or in your community, developing trust and respect, which are essential if your words and actions are to have an impact on them. Look for opportunities to plant seeds in casual conversation as you go about your day; you never know who is listening! Then invite someone to worship; you may be pleasantly surprised to find that all a person needs is a friend who cares enough to ask, a friend who meets them where they are so they can meet Jesus.

However you may be sharing the Gospel, trust that the Holy Spirit's power is at work in you, giving you the words to say and the bold, beautiful feet to demonstrate the Good News in your everyday walk or run.

Dear Lord, You have given me truly beautiful feet to carry Your Good News to the world! Uphold me by Your Spirit, and show me where You would have me run with the Gospel, that others may receive the free gift of salvation by Your grace which is mine in Christ. In His name. Amen.

Big Boots to Fill

Therefore be imitators of God, as beloved children.
And walk in love, as Christ loved us and gave
Himself up for us. Ephesians 5:1–2

I remember giggling as I slipped my small feet into my father's much larger cowboy boots. And I remember my mom running for the camera. What I don't remember was just how young I was. The dated photo provides proof of my tender age of four. It also shows how my pant legs were stretched over Dad's tall boot tops that reached well above my knees. The resulting appearance: a tiny, very bowlegged-looking cowgirl pretending to be her daddy. Those were big boots to fill; they still are. My little tootsies kept slipping and sliding as I struggled to walk, attempting to imitate my father in his size-11 cowboy boots. But I wanted to be like him; I still do.

Although he was not perfect, my father taught me honest living and a hard day's work on the farm. He modeled generosity and mercy as he walked in love, interacting with neighbors and relatives. His faith was sure and steady, shown in his quiet reverence for God as he walked into church every week, clad in those big boots. He listened to the Scriptures and humbly bowed his head in prayer; he heard the message of the sermon and tasted forgiveness through the Sacrament as he knelt at the altar.

My feet are larger now, but I still can't fill my father's boots. I have, however, learned much from him over the years by listening to his careful instruction and observing his life modeled for me. And I hope that my beautiful feet have grown to become more like his.

As I have imitated my dad (and perhaps you also have sought to emulate someone you admire), how much more should we imitate our perfect heavenly Father as His beloved children? In our sin, we slip and slide; we struggle to walk in love toward others. While it is impossible to fill God's big boots, we can rest in the knowledge that He is at work in us, growing us to become more like Him in every way. In His Word, God has proclaimed forgiveness for all our struggles and failures. He has brought us into the way of salvation in Christ, who "loved us and gave Himself up for us." The Holy Spirit fills us and enables us to walk in love toward God and others. He stirs in us the desire to grow in His Word, listen to His careful instruction, and observe Christ in His perfect life modeled for us. Because of His strength, our beautiful feet continue to grow to become more like His!

Heavenly Father, thank You for the people with big boots that You have placed in my life, giving me godly examples I desire to imitate. Through the power of Your Holy Spirit, grow in me; give me the desire to imitate You in every way, walking in love as Christ loved me and gave Himself up for me. In His name I pray. Amen.

Calloused

And I will give you a new heart, and a new spirit I
will put within you. And I will remove the heart of
stone from your flesh and give you a heart of flesh.
Ezekiel 36:26

Wandering through the wilderness had been rough. And long.
Her sandal-clad feet were exposed to the harsh environment
on the entire journey. At first soft and tender, her delicate
young feet had skipped lightly across the parted waters of the
Red Sea. They danced joyfully in praise with other beautiful
feet, their freedom finally secure, as the parted waters closed
in on their former captors. As the journey continued, however,
her feet ached and throbbed; her tender flesh was continually
scraped, and her soles cracked and bled. She cried out in pain.
Over time and over miles of rocky terrain, her once-tender
feet grew tough and calloused. After years of seemingly endless wandering, she ceased to cry out and merely went through
the motions, numb and unfeeling.

This is the imagined picture of a young Hebrew girl during the
time Moses led the Israelites from captivity in Egypt and into
the wilderness. Could this also describe a real picture of you or
me as we gaze at a rough portion of our life's journey?

We skip lightly through life when diplomas are awarded and as
wedding bells ring. Our beautiful feet dance joyfully as careers
soar and when babies are born. As our journey continues,
however, troubles mix with triumphs: prolonged illness,
strained relationships, unemployment, rebellious children, a
loved one's death, and more. We are continually exposed to the

realities of sin and hardship in our own life and in the lives of those we know. Our feelings are hurt and scraped; our emotions are raw and laid bare. We cry out in pain. Over time, as difficulties continue to pile up and the effects of sin take their toll, our once-tender hearts may grow tough and calloused. We may be tempted to build up thick, hard walls around our hearts, fearful of more pain. Like many of the Israelites during their wilderness wandering, we become hardhearted and bitter. Thinking our situation is hopeless, we cease to cry out; we go through the motions of life, numb and unfeeling.

Is our situation hopeless? No! King David, who was suffering from a prolonged illness that threatened death, did not give up, but cried out in agony, "How long, O Lord? Will You forget me forever? How long will You hide Your face from me?" In his next breath, David declared the truth of which he was certain: "But I have trusted in Your steadfast love; my heart shall rejoice in Your salvation" (Psalm 13:1, 5). God had not forgotten David, nor had He hidden His face from him. The same is true for you and for me. The journey is sometimes long and rough; the pain is difficult to bear; and we may be tempted to lose faith. But we can cling to the hope given to us in Christ, who knows our pain and feels our hurt, who walks with us! God's steadfast love for us sent His Son to the cross, securing our freedom from sin. He trades our scarred hearts for new hearts and places His Spirit within us. No longer calloused, our hearts, like David's, rejoice in the Lord's salvation!

Lord Jesus, forgive me for the times when I have allowed the difficulties of life to make me calloused and hardhearted. Fill me with Your Spirit; give me a heart that rejoices continually in Your salvation! Help me to see that You walk with me on my journey. In Your name. Amen.

Cold Feet

Have I not commanded you? Be strong and courageous. Do not be frightened, and do not be dismayed, for the Lord your God is with you wherever you go. Joshua 1:9

The wedding music begins, the guests rise, and the blushing bride marches down the aisle. But where is the groom? In a panic, he has ducked out the back door and has run away from the church instead of saying, "I do." A classic case of cold feet.

We may laugh about this poor fellow's predicament, but perhaps we need to check the temperature of our own tootsies instead. How often do we experience cold feet? When do we "chicken out" of doing something because fear has seized us? How often do we "freeze up" when we find ourselves in a confrontational situation? When do we lose all confidence that we have the ability to complete the task given us?

Satan threatens us with lies like "You can't!" Our own sinful flesh says, "Give up! Run away!" And our feet grow cold. We feel the warm blood rushing away from our lowest extremities when we listen to these lies or fall for the foolish notions that we are incapable of accomplishing what God has called our beautiful feet to do. He has commanded us to be strong and courageous, to meditate on His Word, "careful to do according to all that is written in it" (Joshua 1:8). We are to serve God and others, even if that puts us in strenuous, new, or challenging situations. He tells us to share the Gospel with a world in desperate need of a Savior; perhaps that means reaching out to the neighbor next door or to the tribe in the mission field overseas (gulp!). He calls us to love Him above all else, more than our loved ones or this life. And He commands us to love our neighbors as ourselves—even the unlikable ones.

Are your feet chilling at the mere mention of some of these commands? Perhaps right now you face a specific challenge and your feet are turning to ice. You want to duck out the back door and run away! Instead, turn to God. Confess your cold feet to Him, confident that He hears your prayer and forgives you for Jesus' sake. He has scooped you up and saved you—cold feet and all—wrapping you in His warm embrace, thawing your numb tootsies, turning them toasty warm. He is the ultimate foot warmer! The Lord gives us strength and courage where we are weak and frightened. He is with us wherever we go. His Spirit empowers us to courageously say "I do" to all that He has commanded us to do.

> *Savior Jesus, in my weakness, I become frightened and dismayed. Forgive me for my cold feet, for my failure to serve You or courageously do all You have called me to do. Fill me with Your strength and courage. Warm my beautiful feet that they may be obedient to You. In Your name. Amen.*

Corrective Shoes

I know, O Lord, that the way of man is not in himself, that it is not in man who walks to direct his steps. Correct me, O Lord, but in justice; not in Your anger, lest You bring me to nothing.
Jeremiah 10:23–24

My feet turned inward. "Pigeon-toed," they called it, and the doctor told my parents we needed to correct it before I grew older. Otherwise, my feet would grow more stubborn in their disposition to face each other instead of staring straight ahead, which would cause me to trip over myself as I walked.

At five years of age, I travelled to a special shoe store and sat patiently as the specialist fit my foot to my very own pair of corrective shoes. I even selected the lovely red and blue-colored saddle-style shoes that I would wear every day for the next year! It felt exciting and fun at the time. My feet soon felt otherwise. Those stubborn piggies wanted to go their own way, but when they were placed in this fine footwear, they were noticeably nudged to make a change! The marvel of my corrective shoes, whose purpose was to train my feet not to turn inward, actually turned my feet *out*. This gave the shoes an odd appearance—it looked as though I had my shoes on the wrong feet. When I walked, jumped, skipped, and ran, I felt as though I had my shoes on the wrong feet too!

The correction was painful but necessary. On my own, I could not have made the correction. I could have told my feet to walk straight but they would not have, and I could not have fixed them myself. Today, I'm a runner, and I thank my parents for the necessary correction for my beautiful feet!

Let's face it: we all walk a little (or a lot) pigeon-toed in this life. And God tells us this is an incomparably more serious problem that needs correction! Young or old, we are stubborn in our sinful disposition; we look to ourselves first; we desire to walk our own way even when we know that way is faulty, causing us to trip all over ourselves and others. God desires that we turn straight ahead and follow Him on a path that He directs. But try as we might on our own, we just can't do it. We desperately need correction. And it can't come from within us. Only God can make that change in us, providing just the right correction we so desperately need.

Correction is painful, but oh, so necessary. So we sit patiently (or not so patiently) as our Specialist works with us. In His Word, God shows us our sin; we are convicted of these sins by the sting of the Law, which we cannot keep on our own. He lovingly disciplines us when we have foolishly gone our own way. In His mercy and grace, God chooses us, pigeon-toed, inwardly-focused sinners, and heals us, making a complete correction. And He does all this through the selfless suffering and death of His Son, Jesus Christ. Our sins are forgiven; our salvation is complete! Filled with power from the Holy Spirit, we are able to turn straight ahead and run down the path that He directs, following His lead.

Dear God, I have often walked my own way, pigeon-toed,
tripping along the way. Forgive me for my sinful disposi-
tion. Thank You, heavenly Father, for the necessary
correction in Christ for my beautiful feet. Empower me
to run straight ahead and follow You. In Jesus' precious
name. Amen.

Cross Trainers

> Everyone who competes in the games goes into
> strict training. They do it to get a crown that will
> not last; but we do it to get a crown that will last
> forever. 1 Corinthians 9:25 (NIV)

Slipping my beautiful feet into the latest pair of cross-trainers
at the shoe store, I felt certain I could do just about anything!
This specially engineered athletic shoe was uniquely designed
to provide multidirectional support for the feet as they train
for a variety of sports. I assumed that these shoes would give
me instant ability to perform exercises and sports with ease.
What a bummer to learn that shoes do not the athlete make! If
I were to compete and win a 5K run (or at least keep up with
my aerobics classmates), I needed to go into strict training.

My physical trainer stressed the importance of cross-training,
and I smiled down at my shoes, which were appropriately
named. To continually improve my physical condition and be
ready for competition, he said I should cross-train—engage in
both aerobic activities and strength training—train rigorously
in a variety of sports, strengthening all major muscle groups
and building cardiovascular endurance at the same time.

When the apostle Paul wrote to the church in Corinth, he was
inspired by the Lord to give the people word pictures they
could understand. They knew about competition; the Greeks
gave them the Olympic Games, and they led their own compe-
titions in the Isthmian Games. Competitors strove to win the
prize of a perishable crown or wreath of leaves. Just prior to
the verse above, the apostle Paul wrote, "Do you not know that

in a race all the runners run, but only one gets the prize? Run in such a way as to get the prize" (v. 24 NIV).

The cross-trainers on my feet reminded me of our run with the Lord and the need for strict training. Cross training. As we run through this life, we should do so with the vigor of an athlete. In the variety of activities that we do, we should give our best, use every ounce of energy, hold nothing back as we strain toward the goal to win the prize. That means studying God's Word with fervor, serving Him diligently with our hands and feet, living each day as a bold witness of His love to others, earnestly seeking His will for our lives, praying without ceasing. Cross training.

The problem is that we are weak and sinful. On our own, we slow to a crawl and we fall repeatedly. We are incapable of finishing the competition, let alone striving for the prize. Praise be to God, who picks us up and dusts us off, cleanses us and forgives us in Christ, who bore the cross for us. He enables us to become cross trainers, to take up our crosses daily and follow after Him (Luke 9:23) by the power of His Spirit in us. Wherever we turn, His multidirectional support protects us. He provides us with the strength and the endurance needed to strain toward the goal. And we run, with the Lord by our side, knowing that in Christ, we have already won the prize! Salvation is ours. By His grace, the crown you and I receive—the crown of life—is not perishable, but lasts forever.

Lord Jesus, thank You for bearing the cross, taking my
sins upon Yourself, and forgiving me. By Your Spirit,
continually enable me to be a cross trainer, taking up my
cross daily and following You. In Your name. Amen.

Fabulous or Faulty Footwear

[Jesus said,] "In the world you will have tribulation.
But take heart; I have overcome the world."
John 16:33

As we lift the lids from boxes of fabulous footwear for our beautiful feet, we may find ourselves staring at stylish high heels. Gorgeous, sleek, and shiny, in an amazing array of colors, designs, and details. Beautiful. Do you ever wonder, though, what the shoe designers were thinking when they came up with this style of fabulous footwear (or should I say "faulty" footwear)? One faulty design is the triangular toe. Who has naturally triangular feet? Another fault is those three-, four-, or five-inch heels. They make the toes, legs, and back hurt. Do you ever wonder if supermodels are cringing behind those blank expressions as they stride down the runway?

But admit it. When we want to get really dressed up for work, for church, for a party—what do we wear? High heels. How can high heels make us look so good when they hurt so badly? High heels are proof that we can have beautiful-looking feet on the outside and be hurting on the inside.

Our walk through life has its high-heel moments, doesn't it? Outwardly, everything looks good, beautiful, perfect. Inside, everything feels bad, ugly, painful. At times, we look at other women with envy and think, "Why do they have it all together and I don't? Why do they look so good?" The truth is that we don't know what's taking place in their lives, what's happening on the inside. Yes, on the outside, all can look good. But inside, there may be pain. Hurt feelings and hurt relationships. Illness and loss. Disappointment and anxiety.

Those high-heeled moments of life are indeed painful. What relief when we are finally able to step out of them. So let's take them off to talk about some good news! If you are hurting inside right now, know that you are not alone in your pain. Jesus took on all the pain and sorrow you would ever know when He went to the cross for you. He did not say, "*If* you have tribulation," or, "In the world you *might* have tribulation." He said, "You will."

Yes, we are sinners living in a fallen, sin-filled world. There will be trouble, pain, and hurt in our lives as a result of sin. But we can take heart: Jesus overcame the world—sin, death, and the devil—when He died for us. We can take refuge in Christ, assured of His promise of forgiveness and salvation, which He freely gave on the cross and at the empty tomb. Jesus is our sure hope in the midst of pain. He brings healing to our hurt and suffering. And God uses our high-heeled moments to draw us closer to Him, to help us see our need for a deeper relationship with Him. Limping with pain, we learn to lean more heavily on the One who walks beside us always.

> *Lord Jesus, we praise and thank You that You have over-*
> *come the world, that You took on all the pain and sorrow*
> *we would ever know when You went to the cross for us,*
> *giving us forgiveness and salvation. Please use our high-*
> *heeled moments to draw us closer to You.*
> *In Your name we pray. Amen.*

Faithful Flip-Flops

Do nothing from rivalry or conceit, but in humility
count others more significant than yourselves. Let
each of you look not only to his own interests, but
also to the interests of others. Philippians 2:3–4

Quite possibly my favorite footwear (and perhaps yours too) is
a pair of flip-flops. From a simple plastic top with a rubber sole
to the fancy fabric-covered kind with ornate details, flip-flops
are so fun! I believe women love flip-flops for many reasons,
including their comfort, their cuteness, and their *immediate
availability*. My flip-flops are always by the door, at the ready.

This simple shoe style requires a full two seconds to slip into!
And nothing shows off (or reveals) our beautiful feet any better than faithful flip-flops. We are women on the go, and this
footwear enables us to go *now*! We are ready at a moment's
notice to lend a helping hand to a neighbor, to run a meal to a
family in need. We drop everything to respond to a community crisis or to offer our God-given gifts to our congregation.
We slide into our sandals to drop off our kids or grandkids,
tending to their needs. We run errands for others—everything
from groceries to garage sales. We walk beside someone who
would otherwise walk alone. Clad in our fabulous flip-flops,
we step out to serve at a moment's notice, ready and willing to
serve our loved ones and our Lord.

When we slip *into* this footwear and step *out* to serve, we
humbly allow ourselves to be immediately available to others,
which causes us to invest in our relationships more and dwell
on ourselves less. If we are busy serving the people around us,

we are less absorbed with ourselves: *our* personal appearances, *our* feelings, *our* desires, *our* schedules, *our* self-interests.

Sadly, we live in a sin-filled world that continually tells us to look out for number one, to take care of our own needs first, to look only to our own interests and not to the interests of others, going completely against God's commands (see v. 4 above). Our sinful human nature is full of conceit; it is totally self-centered and self-seeking. Praise God for His perfect love and forgiveness in Christ. He cleanses us of our conceit and saves us from our self-centeredness. Through the power of His Holy Spirit, He enables us and prepares us to "slip in" and serve others in selfless love, counting them more significant than ourselves.

Where do you see an immediate need around you right now? After taking two seconds to slip into this fun footwear, how could you possibly meet that need? However you are serving, remember that the Lord is equipping your beautiful feet with faithful flip-flops, providing you with immediate availability as you step out to serve!

> *Dear God, thank You for providing me with opportunities to humbly serve others as I slip into the faithful footwear that gives me immediate availability. Empower me to step out to serve now in my beautiful feet! In Jesus' name. Amen.*

Foot-bound or Footloose?

So if the Son sets you free, you will be free indeed.
John 8:36

During a college course in American history, my class was discussing the Civil War and the abolishment of slavery in the South. One misguided young student defiantly rose to her feet, proclaiming the injustice of the decision to abolish slavery. She insisted that slavery was necessary to the economy of the South and that slaves were not mistreated, as commonly thought, but quite happy in their existence. She sat down as abruptly as she had stood, and the room was filled with an uncomfortable silence. After a moment of careful thought, the professor shook her head sadly and gently but firmly rebuked this young woman, informing her that human bondage was not something to be desired and certainly not to be prized!

Human bondage. Shackled feet, bound and chained to prevent the slave from escaping. Our nation's museums display shackles and other items used in forced slave labor; drawings and paintings depict the buying and selling of slaves, chained and shackled; all are grim reminders of this cruel part of our past. Stories are shared about slaves who were carried to freedom until their emancipators could find a way to cut the shackles from their beautiful feet so they could be set free. Can you imagine how that must have felt, having lived a life in chains and now being freed from bondage? liberated from a life of captivity? released from the bonds of slavery? Feet that were formerly bound were now cut loose. Footloose and free!

Although we may have never known the pain of that kind of human bondage, although we can thank God that our feet never knew the sting of shackles as they scraped against our skin and bound us against our will, although we were never the property of another human being—we were slaves. Ours was a fate far worse than human slavery, for we were bound for hell; we were lost and condemned, slaves to sin and its power over us. Jesus said, "Truly, truly, I say to you, everyone who commits sin is a slave to sin" (John 8:34). Held captive by our selfish thoughts and words, bound by our fears and failures as slaves to our evil desires and deeds, we stumbled through this life, shackled in sin with no way to free ourselves. And then, our Emancipator came and carried us to freedom! Jesus Christ, God's Son, cut away the shackles of sin that held us in bondage. In His glorious death and resurrection, He liberated us, once and for all, from a life of captivity to sin. Foot-bound no longer, we are footloose and free! Liberated! Emancipated! Glory be to God, whose Son has set us free. We are free indeed!

Lord Jesus Christ, I confess that I have been a slave to sin. But You have found me and carried me to freedom, cutting away the shackles that bound me. Strengthen me by Your Spirit to live my life for You. In Your name. Amen.

Foot-in-Mouth Syndrome

Even a fool who keeps silent is considered
wise; when he closes his lips,
he is deemed intelligent. Proverbs 17:28

"Are they both your sons?" inquired the store manager,
motioning behind me. I stared blankly at her and then turned
to look back at my husband and four-year-old son, who waited
in line with me at the checkout.

"Excuse me?" I asked, thinking I had misheard her. (Could
I possibly look old enough to be my husband's mother?) My
bewildered expression must have caused her to realize she had
erred. "Well, you just never know these days. I mean—" and
she rambled, inserting both feet further into her mouth.

"This is my husband, and this is my son," I calmly corrected,
pointing to each in turn.

We all have embarrassing foot-in-mouth tales to tell, don't we?
I once announced that the young man in our church's youth
group had "checked me out." Noticing several raised eyebrows,
I quickly tried to pry my foot out of my mouth by explaining
that he had been the staff person for the church rummage sale
checkout.

Open mouth; insert foot. There is danger involved every time
we open our mouths to speak. Because I love to speak and
feel the need to share thousands of words daily with anyone
who will listen, I would be wise to heed the many words from
Proverbs on this subject. The following is just a sampling:

When words are many, sin is not absent, but he
who holds his tongue is wise. (10:19 NIV)
Reckless words pierce like a sword, but the tongue
of the wise brings healing. (12:18 NIV)
A wise man's heart guides his mouth, and his lips
promote instruction. (16:23 NIV)

What can you and I learn from these verses? A wise person
carefully chooses words, guided by her heart, that promote
healing and instruction. Even a fool with closed lips can be
thought wise and intelligent (Proverbs 17:28), so shouldn't we
consider holding our tongues, carefully weighing our words
before they are spoken?

These are wonderful words of wisdom, but there is still one
big, foot-shaped problem. We do not possess the ability to
use this wisdom on our own. Our many words are, instead,
sinful and reckless. Much worse than mere moments of foot-
in-mouth syndrome, our words get us into real trouble; they
can hurt, deceive, and destroy, revealing our sinful hearts
within. Only through God's free gift of forgiveness and mercy
in Christ and through the power of His Spirit at work in our
hearts can our mouths then utter "only such as is good for
building up, as fits the occasion, that it may give grace to those
who hear" (Ephesians 4:29). In His strength, our beautiful feet
remain beneath us where they belong, and not in our mouths.

*Dear God, my words are often sinful and reckless. For
Jesus' sake, forgive me for failing to curb my tongue.
Continually fill my heart with Your Spirit, that my tongue
would be able to declare Your praises, to promote heal-
ing and instruction. May my words bless all who hear. In
Jesus' holy name. Amen.*

Get Your Foot in the Door

> I have become all things to all people, that by all
> means I might save some. I do it all for the sake of
> the gospel, that I may share with them in its bless-
> ings. 1 Corinthians 9:22–23

Stories are told of traveling salesmen, back in the days when goods like vacuum cleaners, toiletries, magazines, and more were sold door-to-door. "Ma'am, if I could just have a few minutes of your time, I have a product that will make your life so much easier!" SLAM! House after house, doors were slammed in their faces before they had a chance to pitch their amazing products. A savvy sales technique was soon born: the door-to-door salesman was instructed to literally put his foot in the door the moment it was opened so the door could not be closed. This method worked quite well. The homemaker, unable to get rid of a salesman so easily, would be forced to listen to the sales pitch and often became a buying customer.

The sales technique became so well known that it grew into a catch phrase used to describe situations where a person is confident that her ideas will be positively received if she can first get noticed or heard. If she is just given a chance! If she can just "get her foot in the door."

As Christians seeking to share the message of salvation in Christ with the world around us, we are not pitching a product or trying to convince people to buy into something. We *are* trying to tell them the most important words they will ever hear: "Sir, if I could just have a few minutes of your time? You have a Savior named Jesus who died for you; He gives you life and—" SLAM! Some people walk away, cover their ears, or slam the door before we have a chance to tell them what they need to hear. We know that the Gospel is compelling, if only others would listen. So we can take a lesson from the savvy salesman: we first need to get our beautiful feet in the door! I'm not suggesting that we literally force our feet through the doorways of people's homes. Getting your foot in the door with the Gospel means getting to know people first, gaining their trust and respect. Your words will be more positively received when you have established a relationship with them.

By the power of the Holy Spirit, you can be an effective witness. Show a genuine interest in people's lives and concerns; be respectful of differences while maintaining your integrity and not compromising faith or values. Meet people where they are and walk alongside them. Then, don't be surprised if, over time, they begin to take notice or give you a chance by listening when you share His Word with them. "Do it all for the sake of the Gospel"—the Good News of salvation in Christ that we, too, received by the grace of God, who forgives us even when we slam the door on His message.

God fills you and me with faith and strength to share His Word and the blessings that come from the Gospel. He uses our humble work to touch people's hearts and save them by His grace. The Spirit reveals to them through the Word that they cannot live without their Savior, Jesus Christ.

Dear God, thank You for the Gospel and the blessing of salvation that is mine in Christ! Guide me to get my foot in the door with others, that by Your power, my words would be positively received as I share Your Word. In Jesus' name. Amen.

Goody Two-Shoes

For I am not ashamed of the gospel,
for it is the power of God for salvation to
everyone who believes. Romans 1:16

"What a Goody Two-shoes!" came the familiar mocking words. They had been whispered behind her back more than a few times, spoken just loud enough so she would hear. As she continued down the hall of her high school, another remark was flung in her direction: "I bet she thinks she's perfect too."

Ouch. If only they knew! She was well aware of her past struggles with self-confidence. The lies she told to make herself sound appealing to the other kids. The impure thoughts that had previously plagued her mind. The unhealthy relationships she had fallen into, just to fit in somewhere. But then something happened that had changed everything. It was the words the pastor had said on that Sunday many months ago, when she had reluctantly gone to church. He said that no matter what you have done, no matter what mistakes you have made, you are never beyond the reach of God's grace. He forgives you by the death and resurrection of His perfect Son, Jesus Christ, and claims you as His own precious child. Chosen by Him and covered by His blood, you are made perfect in Christ; your confidence and your identity come from who you are in Him!

She felt that God had reached down and covered her completely with His perfect grace and forgiveness, filling her with the Holy Spirit and giving her a peace beyond compare! By the Spirit's power, she began to think and behave differently. She walked with a new confidence; she knew she was something special in Christ. No longer feeling the need to lie, she became more open and honest with her peers and sought healthier relationships. Although she sometimes still stumbled, she knew now that His grace was there to catch her if she should fall. Knowing she had been forgiven for so much more, she found it easier to forgive others, even when they made mocking remarks like, "There goes Little Miss Christian!" She looked down at her two beautiful feet. Goody Two-shoes? Hardly. Made perfect in Christ? Absolutely!

The story of this teenage girl reminds us that when a life is changed in Christ, the world may not respond too kindly. The unbelieving world may take offense and poke fun at us when we, empowered by the Spirit, live our lives in God-pleasing ways. Satan works hard to hinder our witness to the world, but we can take heart because God is so much more powerful! He will strengthen us and enable us to stand strong in our faith, unashamed of the Good News of Christ and its power to save!

Maybe your story is similar to hers. Forgiven and chosen in Christ, you walk by faith in your two good shoes; your feet are "fitted with the readiness that comes from the gospel of peace" (Ephesians 6:15 NIV). And yet, you are made fun of and criticized. Although the world may call you Goody Two-shoes, stand strong knowing He can use you to bring the Gospel to the world in need of a Savior.

Dear Lord, I praise You for Your grace, which covers me.
You forgive me no matter what; I am made perfect in
Christ! Strengthen me by Your Spirit that I may walk by
faith, unashamed of the Gospel and its power to save.
In Jesus' name. Amen.

Make Tracks!

"Then go quickly and tell His disciples that He has risen from the dead. . . . " So they departed quickly from the tomb with fear and great joy, and ran to tell His disciples. Matthew 28:7–8

Their steps were slow and heavy, but the grieving women's feet carried them dutifully toward the tomb, where their Lord Jesus' body had been laid to rest only a few days earlier. All of the sudden, the ground shook, the stone was rolled back from the tomb, and an angel dressed in brilliant light appeared, seated on the stone. The angel said to the women, "Go quickly and tell His disciples that He has risen." Risen?! Jesus had risen? They must make tracks! They must waste no time! This was urgent news, and it must be told *now*! Grief turned instantly to joy, and the women's steps were suddenly quick and light as they ran to tell the good news.

Jesus gives us a similar command, and there is no time to waste! "Go . . . and make disciples of all nations" (Matthew 28:19). We can put our feet up and say, "Let someone else make tracks. I'm going to stay put." Do we sit idly by while a world is dying without knowledge or faith in their risen Savior? Although we sit carelessly in our sin, failing to heed His commands, God never fails us! The Gospel message He commands us to share is meant for our ears too.

You may wonder, "But how can I make tracks?" Empowered by the Spirit, you can make a world of difference to the world. Make tracks to your local homeless shelter and lend a helping hand. Be the hands and feet of Jesus to members of your community who have recently faced hardship; deliver a meal, send a card, or give them something of yours that they may need, expecting nothing in return. Go quickly to your church and jump in to serve, using your God-given gifts. Maybe you can teach children or serve in the kitchen. Perhaps you can make a joyful noise in the choir or serve on a mission trip. Make tracks every time you step out the door, knowing that time is short and the world outside your door needs to know it has a risen Savior. In every conversation and every interaction, you have the opportunity to represent Jesus. Show His grace; tell of His great mercy and forgiveness; live a life of love, as He loved us and gave Himself up for us that we can have eternal life in Him.

Make tracks. Get going—and quickly. This is urgent news and it must be told now! When you run quickly with your beautiful feet to a world in need of a Savior, the only thing you leave behind are your tracks. How wonderful that your tracks remain, giving someone else your footprints to follow that they may go and do likewise! Your example of selfless serving and sacrifice leaves an impression for other beautiful feet to fill.

Lord Jesus, show me how and where You would have me make tracks today! Fill me and strengthen me, that I may boldly represent You, sharing salvation in Your name to the world. You are risen! Alleluia! In Your name I pray. Amen.

Making a Statement

For God gave us a spirit not of fear but of power
and love and self-control. 2 Timothy 1:7

Heads turn and all eyes are on our beautiful feet as we walk
into work, into school, into the mall—sporting our latest pair
of phenomenal footwear. Maybe it's a pair of shiny red pumps
or rhinestone-studded flip-flops that say "Bling!" as we walk
by. Perhaps it's that pair of retro platform shoes making their
return to the fashion world or those fun sneakers with lights
that flash with every step. Regardless of our choice, when we
are sporting festive footwear, we are boldly making a statement!

If our shoes can make a statement that causes heads to turn
and people to take notice, how much more can our lives make
a statement that attracts attention as we walk with the Lord?
Attention that draws people not to us, but to Christ through
us, that He would be glorified and that they would see His
love.

Do you make that statement? Without saying a word, is your
life speaking loud and clear to the world around you that you
belong to Christ? Or are you afraid to make a statement for
fear that you will trip and fall or that the statement you make
will appear unpopular or out-of-date? In our sin, we are fearful
and weak. We fail to make any statement at all. But Jesus made
the ultimate statement by showing the extent of His love for us
when He stretched out His arms and died for the forgiveness
of our sins. He has chosen us, and He gives us the Holy Spirit,
filling us with the Spirit's "power and love and self-control."

By His Spirit, you can make a statement with your life. In His love, let someone go ahead of you in the long line at the grocery store. Pay for the meal at the table next to yours or for the car behind yours in the drive-through lane. Mow the neighbors' lawn when they least expect it. Try some other random acts of kindness, like delivering groceries or baked goods to someone who could really use a pick-me-up. With His power and strength, turn the other cheek. Squelch gossip. Say no to something that would get in the way of your commitment to attend church. Pray for others, and let them know you are doing it.

People are always watching—and listening. As Christian women, our lives make bold, powerful statements and speak volumes to the world around us that we belong to the Lord.

As you live your life for an audience of One, seeking to serve and please the Lord with your actions, others take notice. They see that you are different. The Lord will use your life to touch theirs with His saving love in Christ.

> *Dear Jesus, forgive me for my fear and weakness that keep me from making a statement for You. Thank You for filling me with Your Spirit, providing me with Your power and love and self-control so I can make a bold statement with my life as I walk with You. In Your name. Amen.*

Putting Your Foot Down

My son, do not despise the LORD's discipline or be
weary of His reproof, for the LORD reproves him
whom He loves, as a father the son in whom he
delights. Proverbs 3:11–12

"No, you may not have candy for supper. I've told you a
hundred times: it is not a vegetable and it will not make
you grow!" "Yes, you will go to school today, even though
you don't like your haircut." "I'm sorry; you can't watch that
R-rated movie." "Yes, you will apologize to her; what you did
was wrong." "No, you may not attend the party with no adult
supervision." "Yes, you will join us for worship." "That's final.
I'm putting my foot down."

As parents or people in authority, there are times we have to
put our foot down. We have established important rules. On
given issues, we have to take a stance, make a wise decision
on behalf of our growing children, and stand by that decision
even when it is not very popular because we know it is in their
best interest. We guide, direct, and discipline out of delight
and love for our children. It is from this guidance that they
grow and mature, gain the ability to discern right from wrong,
and build healthy habits and lasting relationships. And when
the rules are broken, we must reprove them, teaching them
there are consequences to their disobedience.

How wonderful that God, in His perfect parental love for us,
puts His foot down! His Word is very clear; we do not have to
wonder what His stance is on any given issue. Sometimes His
rules and directives are not very popular with us. We would

rather go our own way and do as we think best. We are not unlike a rebellious child refusing instruction. We "despise the LORD's discipline." But He has our best interest in mind. As He guides us in His Word, He says, "No, you shall have no other gods before Me—not those trinkets that you treasure or your desire to put yourselves first." "No, you will not take My name in vain. My name is holy; use it only out of reverence for Me." "Yes, you will remember the Sabbath." "And yes, you will honor your parents." "No, you may not murder or commit adultery or steal or lie! And no coveting, either—of anything." "That's final. I'm putting My foot down."

God's Ten Commandments were given out of love for His children. Rebellious children that we are, we cannot keep them! On our own, we break God's rules; we are incapable and unwilling to receive His guidance and direction. His Law shows us our sin and our need for a Savior. So God put His foot down again. In perfect love, Christ willingly put His beautiful feet down on the rough wood of the cross to be pierced for our sins. Jesus bled and died for our rebellion and disobedience. His death and resurrection secured our salvation. Chosen in Christ and filled with faith, we are enabled by His Spirit to grow in God's Word, to gain the strength we need to cling to what is right and resist what is wrong. We delight in the Lord's discipline, for great is His love for us.

Father God, thank You for putting Your foot down. Upheld by Your Spirit, may I not despise Your discipline but delight in it, knowing that You have my best interest in mind and that Your love for me is so great that You sent Your Son to die for me. In Jesus' name. Amen.

Servant Sandals

As each has received a gift, use it to serve one another, as good stewards of God's varied grace: . . .
whoever serves, as one who serves by the strength
that God supplies—in order that in everything God
may be glorified through Jesus Christ.
1 Peter 4:10–11

In Bible times, people wore a basic style of sandal: leather laces
strapped to a leather bottom. It was simple yet appropriate for
the often hot, dry climate, providing just enough protection
for the bottom of the foot. Sandals were left by the door of the
house, so strapping on sandals meant a person was heading
out, ready for action. Ready to serve.

Such was the case when Moses strapped on his sandals to
lead God's children out of Egypt and across the miraculously
parted waters of the Red Sea. He didn't know he was in for a
forty-year journey in his footwear! Moses' beautiful feet faithfully led the Israelites back and forth across the wilderness for
four decades. [Moses said,] "I have led you forty years in the
wilderness. Your clothes have not worn out on you, and your
sandals have not worn off your feet" (Deuteronomy 29:5).

Incredible! If we could get that kind of wear out of sandals
today, shoe stores would be out of business! Can you hear the
shoe salesman? "Trust me, you don't want that pair with the
forty-year guarantee; they are way too dependable, far too
sturdy!" Obviously, the durability of the Israelites' footwear
had everything to do with God's miraculous provision and
not the quality of the sandals, but this makes me think about

a very special purpose for slipping our feet into these servant shoes: sandals remind us of commitment and perseverance.

Moses was on a mission to lead God's people out of slavery and into the Promised Land. Strengthened by God, Moses' constant commitment to serve and obey the Lord enabled Him to persevere, as the Israelites repeatedly grumbled and complained, failed to trust, and fell away. Not only did their feet wander all over the desert, but their hearts also wandered far from the Lord. Time and time again, Moses' servant sandals led them back to the right path as he pleaded to God on their behalf and God was merciful to them. God was glorified through Moses' service.

In our sin, we are more like the faithless, grumbling Israelites than the faithful servant Moses. We fall away and fail to trust; our hearts wander far from the Lord. On the cross, Jesus pleaded to God on our behalf and God was merciful, forgiving us and filling us with His faith-giving Spirit, our source of strength!

Through countless and sometimes thankless acts of service, we are strengthened by the Lord with the ability to stick to it, to stay committed, and to persevere, much as Moses did! We serve with commitment and perseverance when we patiently care for aging parents, when we struggle to raise godly children, when we teach Sunday School to a dozen feisty children who act as though they aren't listening! Where do you serve with commitment and perseverance? Rely on the strength God supplies, that He may be glorified in Christ!

> *Dear Lord, thank You for equipping me with servant*
> *sandals for my beautiful feet, giving me Your strength for*
> *the long road of service ahead. May You be glorified in all*
> *I do! In Jesus' name. Amen.*

Slipper Solace

Be still, and know that I am God. Psalm 46:10

When you slip your tootsies into a soft, warm, fuzzy pair of slippers, what do you want to do? Do you curl up with a good book? relax with a cup of hot cocoa in front of a fireplace? watch a chick flick? Maybe you just want to lounge around the house, enjoying a time of no restrictions, no demands, and no schedule. If you have a favorite, old, well-worn pair of slippers, you know they provide relaxation and rest to your tired, worn-out, swollen feet! They are like a fuzzy, warm embrace, providing much-needed comfort and soothing rest.

God invites us to a time of rest. He desires that we rest in His presence—that we step out of our hurting high heels, our servant sandals, and other fast-paced footwear—and that we slip our beautiful feet into the soothing comfort of slippers. Times of slipper solace are critical to our spiritual health. As Christian women walking with the Lord, we need quiet time in God's Word and in prayer to Him. How is your slipper-time solace these days? Do you know how to be still before the Lord? He wants you to slow down and put your feet up, to take time to shut out the clamor of the world that is always in a hurry, telling you to pick up the pace.

We live in a rushed society that is tapping its toes in an impatient frenzy, expecting us to do yet one more thing. And the problem is that we are often at the heart of the hurry—rushing and racing to accomplish one more task, not stopping long enough to catch our breath, let alone spend precious time with the Lord. We fail to slow down to listen to our Savior's voice. If we did, we would hear Him whisper, "Be still, and know that I am God." We cannot find slipper solace on our own, but only by the grace of God. He lovingly reaches out to us and takes away our failures and our frenzy, forgiving us through the work of His Son on the cross, giving us His peace, the promise of eternal life, and the gift of the Holy Spirit.

Guided and strengthened by the Spirit, you can find a time and place in your day in which you commit to drop everything and find rest in the Lord. And you can offer the same slipper solace of calm and rest to a friend. Pray *with* her and *for* her, asking the Holy Spirit to lead and guide her into a time of rest. Hold her hand and listen with gentleness and kindness through a difficult time. Encourage her to "be still" before the Lord, who provides the cushioning comfort of His love and grace found in His Word.

Dear Heavenly Father, forgive me for my frenzied pace,
for my failure to "be still." Strengthened by the Spirit, may
I rest in Your presence during a slipper solace time each
day. As I do, grow me and guide me in Your Word, that
I may offer the same solace to another. In Jesus' name.
Amen.

Steel-Toed Work Boots

The name of the LORD is a strong tower;
the righteous man runs into it and is safe.
Proverbs 18:10

Strong. Sturdy. Securing. Steel-toed work boots are con-
structed with layers of thick leather, heavy soles, and metal
reinforcement for extra protection. Now that's some kind of
footwear—just not typically *my* kind. When I envision slipping
my beautiful feet into a fabulous new style of footwear, I do
not picture a big, sturdy pair of steel-toed work boots. (I look
for something a little more on the feminine side to properly
accessorize my latest fashion find.) But when I think about my
walk with the Lord and those areas of life in which I find myself weak and wanting, fearful and frightened, suddenly these
handsome work boots sound like just the right style!

The steel-toed work boot is a strong shelter for the foot! Laced
up tightly, nothing but the intended appendage can enter.
Should a heavy tool or piece of equipment fall on the boot, the
foot remains unharmed, safely protected by the strength of the
footwear that completely surrounds and shields the foot from
injury. What a mighty piece of footwear! Can you imagine the
machinist or construction worker facing a day of work without
this kind of protection?

"The name of the LORD is a strong tower"! He delivers us from
all our sins through the cross of Christ, and through Him,
we have right standing before God; we are made righteous
in Christ! By the power of the Holy Spirit, we call upon His
name, our fortress and our strength. We run to our Strong

Tower, and He covers us completely, securing perfect shelter for you and for me from the storms of life, from the evil one who preys on our weaknesses, and from our enemies who threaten to overtake us and turn us away from our faith. Our almighty God gives us strength where we are weak; He is our refuge, our ever-present help, when we are in trouble (Psalm 46:1). By His grace, He completely surrounds us with the courage we need to stand strong. Although temptation, danger, and evil may lurk at the door, we are shielded safely inside His tower, and nothing can harm us spiritually or take us away from the all-powerful love of our Lord. "Neither death nor life, nor angels nor rulers, nor things present nor things to come, nor powers, nor height nor depth, nor anything else in all creation, will be able to separate us from the love of God in Christ Jesus our Lord" (Romans 8:38–39).

Because of the mighty protection that the steel-toed work boot can offer to my beautiful feet, I may have to run out and buy myself a pair, just so I can look down and be continually reminded of the incomparably mightier God I have! Can you imagine facing a day of life without His protection? Thanks to our Strong Tower, we will never have to!

> *Oh Lord, You are my fortress and my strength! Thank You for making me righteous in Christ, filling me with Your Spirit, that I may call upon Your name and run to You, my Strong Tower! In Jesus' name. Amen.*

Stumbling in the Dark

Jesus answered, "Are there not twelve hours in
the day? If anyone walks in the day, he does not
stumble, because he sees the light of this world.
But if anyone walks in the night, he stumbles,
because the light is not in him." John 11:9–10

The babies were crying again, hungry for their 2 a.m. meal.
(Or was it 3 a.m. or 4 a.m.?) My mother, who had graciously
offered to stay with us the first few weeks following their
births, was on the night shift, giving me welcomed rest. Hear-
ing the babies' cries, she stumbled out of bed, weary from too
many sleepless nights, and headed groggily for the nursery.
Thinking it unnecessary to turn on the lights, she headed
through the living room and toward the hall, misjudged her
steps, and jammed her foot squarely into the corner of the
sofa—stubbing her toes painfully in the process and possibly
even breaking one. In the hours and days that followed, her
toes swelled and turned shades of dark purple, black, and blue.
Her limp served to remind us that it would be wise to flip on
the light switch during night-shift feedings because we cannot
see where we are going in the dark.

Unless you are equipped with superhero night vision (and I'm
guessing you aren't), you cannot see in the dark, either. None
of us can. Light is vital to life for many reasons; one is to keep
our beautiful feet from stumbling. We need light—the physical
light in this world with which we see and, more important,
the spiritual light of this world, through whom we receive life.
Sadly, in our sin, we have attempted to function in spiritual

darkness. We have tried to go about our tasks, live our lives, and walk through each day without the Light—completely in the dark. We grope about, stumbling because we cannot see the path ahead of us. Our feet are helpless to provide direction or guidance; they are at our mercy as we propel them forward, sometimes straight into an obstacle. We cry out in pain as we stub our feelings, break our relationships, and hurt those we care about most. In our sin, we choose the darkness over the Light because we know that the choices we have made are evil and we do not want them exposed (John 3:20). But our deeds done in darkness cause our feet to stumble "because the light is not in [us]" (John 11:10).

Jesus said, "I am the light of the world. Whoever follows Me will not walk in darkness, but will have the light of life" (John 8:12). Jesus came to bring light into our dark world. He chose us, calling us "out of darkness into His marvelous light" (1 Peter 2:9), cleansing us of our sins, our evil choices, and our deeds (which have caused us to stumble), healing us where we are stubbed and broken. Filling us with His Spirit, His light shines in our hearts, giving us "the light of the knowledge of the glory of God in the face of Jesus Christ" (2 Corinthians 4:6). He enables us to see the path before us, and He provides all the direction and guidance we need in the light of His Word. By His power, we walk in the light, sharing the light of the world with a world in need of a Savior.

Lord Jesus, shine Your light in me that I may never walk
in darkness. Guide me by the light of Your Word and
empower me to share the light of Your love with others.
In Your name. Amen.

Swept Off Your Feet

How great is the love the Father has lavished on
us, that we should be called children of God!
And that is what we are! 1 John 3:1 (NIV)

The honeymoon was over and we arrived at our new little
home. I had teased my sweetheart that traditionally, the groom
carries the bride over the threshold of their new dwelling as
they enter for the first time. (I did not think he would actually
do it!) But as we stepped up to the door, he stopped suddenly,
turned, looked at me adoringly, and scooped me up—sweeping me off my feet! It wasn't quite as romantic as I had seen
in the movies, since my five-foot, nine-inch frame made it
difficult for him to maneuver me through the door and up
the stairs. When he plopped me down, he was gasping for air;
apparently, it had not been quite as romantic as he had hoped,
either.

Ah, but my husband *did* sweep me off my feet in the romantic sense that every young woman would hope for. As he
courted me, he treated me with special affection, showering
me with gifts, though I did not deserve them and he could
not afford them. Wearing his heart on his sleeve, he made it
very apparent in front of others that I was something special.
He drove hours just to be near me during our long-distance
courtship. Hand in hand, we took long walks and talked
about the dreams for the future that we would share. And
frequently, he professed his love for me. My future husband
lavished his love on me. Smitten and swooning, I was swept
off my feet.

How much greater is the love of your heavenly Father for you! "As the bridegroom rejoices over the bride, so shall your God rejoice over you" (Isaiah 62:5). The Lord meets you right where you are—in the midst of your sin, undeserving of His love—and He looks at you adoringly (yes, *adoringly*) and rejoices over you. He scoops you up, sweeping you off your feet as He holds you in His arms and loves you just as you are. He claims you as His own dear child, forgiving you and cleansing you by the blood of Christ, who died that you might have life with Him forever.

Yes, God lavishes His love on you! He showers you with every good and perfect gift (James 1:17), provides for your every need, pours out blessings beyond measure. His affection for you is revealed plainly for the world to see in the words of His love letter—His Word—written for you. You are something special! He could move mountains just to be near you, but He doesn't have to; He is with you every moment; His Spirit lives in you (1 Corinthians 2:12). He holds you in the palm of His hand (Isaiah 41:13); He listens as you talk about your hope in Him and your future shared in heaven. And always, in every way, He professes His love for you. The perfect love story!

> *Father God, how great is Your love for me! You lavish it*
> *upon me more than a bridegroom for his bride. Fill me*
> *with Your Spirit and lead me to relish Your love letter*
> *written for me, that I may grow in Your love every day.*
> *In Your Son's name I pray. Amen.*

The Beautiful Feet of Jesus

Have this mind among yourselves, which is yours
in Christ Jesus, who, though He was in the form
of God, did not count equality with God a thing to
be grasped, but made Himself nothing, taking the
form of a servant. Philippians 2:5–7

During His earthly ministry, Jesus' feet took Him many
places—through crowded cities, across the open countryside,
over mountains, through winding valleys, across the rugged
terrain of Israel, and even onto the raging waters of the Sea of
Galilee. Every step Jesus took was filled with purpose: bringing
hope, faith, and forgiveness; providing healing, peace, and joy
to people everywhere.

His feet brought Him, one last time, into the city of Jerusalem. It was the evening of the Passover and the Last Supper,
which Jesus was about to share with His disciples. He knew
His time had come; He would soon return to His Father in
heaven. Later that night, He would be betrayed and arrested;
the next day, beaten and crucified. His beautiful feet would
be pierced. Nails would be driven into them. As the Scripture
says, He was "pierced for our transgressions" (Isaiah 53:5
NIV).

That night, before Jesus died for the sins of the whole world,
during the Passover meal, He began to wash the disciples'
feet. After He had finished, He said these words: "Do you
understand what I have done to you? You call Me Teacher
and Lord, and you are right, for so I am. If I then, your Lord
and Teacher, have washed your feet, you also ought to wash

one another's feet. For I have given you an example, that you should do just as I have done to you" (John 13:12-15).

Traveling in the Holy Land was dirty business for feet. Sand and dust blew and were kicked up constantly. Entering a home meant removing one's sandals. And then, the lowest servant of the house would perform a foot washing on those disgustingly grimy feet.

Jesus, Teacher and Lord, took on the lowly servant's role and did this for His disciples in an enormous gesture of love and service. He was about to *die* for them, and here He was, washing their feet, setting an example for them to serve others as He first served them.

Just as Jesus washed the disciples' feet, so He washed us in the waters of Baptism with new birth in the Spirit, giving us faith. He cleansed us of all our sin by His death on the cross so we might be saved. In response to His incredible saving love, empowered by the Holy Spirit, we willingly serve one another as Jesus taught us to do. In humility, we can place others' needs ahead of our own (Philippians 2:3). With servant hearts, we perform those lowly tasks and labor that might be humbling. We make meals, scrub floors, wipe noses, and clean up others' messes. We pray for our friends as well as our enemies. We continue to teach the Gospel, even when it seems no one is listening. We forgive others, even when they are unrepentant. We meet others' needs, even when it means sacrificing some of our own. By God's grace, we serve just as Jesus did!

Dear Jesus, Your feet are truly beautiful! You humbly took the form of a servant and willingly went to the cross, dying that I might have life. Give me servant feet by Your Holy Spirit, that I may humbly serve others as You have taught me to do. In Your name. Amen.

The Path Less Traveled

Jesus said to him, "I am the way, and the truth,
and the life. No one comes to the Father
except through Me." John 14:6

While hiking with my husband on the trail around the base
of the Grand Tetons, I could see the fork in the path ahead.
Clearly, the lower trail was the one chosen by most—clear and
wide, easy to follow. But we were intrigued by the path less
traveled and ventured there on our own, up a much narrower
trail. Although the path was rougher and steeper, we shared an
unexpected adventure and were awed at the sight of a beautiful hidden lake—a view we would surely have missed if we had
stayed on the main trail.

Sometimes walking on the path God chooses for us means
taking the path less traveled or even blazing a whole new
trail. Following the footsteps of the crowd would certainly be
easier, and in our sin, we sometimes do just that. We choose
the lower trail, the path of least resistance. We place our trust
in ourselves to find the way. We allow the world to define our
values; we make crowd-pleasing decisions that do not honor
God; we even fail to stand up for our faith. Despite our sinful
steps down the worldly path, God does not give up on us. In
His love, He sent His Son to die for our sins, cleansing us from
our worldly ways and filling us with faith to follow Him.

As the Holy Spirit leads, we step off the beaten path and take
the narrow, winding way instead. This is the way the world
finds unappealing. The way that trusts God to provide, even
when the numbers in our checkbook aren't "crunching" very

well. The path that refuses to watch popular TV shows that try to redefine our moral values. The way that makes choices for our children that may not be outwardly cool or crowd pleasing. The way that stands up for our faith and our Savior in situations where God's Word is called into question.

Although the world continues to try and redefine our beliefs, wanting us to fall for the lie that all roads lead to heaven, by the power of the Holy Spirit in us, we trust the truth of God's Word that tells us otherwise. Jesus said, "I am the way. . . . No one comes to the Father except through Me." No other roads or paths lead to salvation—to eternity in heaven with our Savior.

Taking the way less traveled, we can't always see what lies ahead on the path as we step out with our beautiful feet; sometimes His path for us is rough and steep and rocky; it may even look scary. But that forces us to trust the maker of the path. As we follow His lead, we are in for an adventure! We know that with every step we take, He has walked before us, making our way clear. As we walk, He also walks beside us. When we stumble, He catches us and steadies us. And when we can no longer stand, He picks us up and carries us. He knows the length of our walk, the end of our journey in this life, and the endless walk we will share with Him in eternity! We will most certainly be awed at the sight of heaven, a view we would have missed on the main trail. By God's grace, I'm taking the path less traveled. How about you?

> *Dear God, forgive me for walking a worldly path instead of following You. By Your Spirit, lead me down the path less traveled; I know my Savior walks beside me. In His name. Amen.*

The Perfect Fit

Having gifts that differ according to the grace
given to us, let us use them. Romans 12:6

What size shoes do your beautiful feet require? When shopping for footwear, it is imperative that the shoes you select are the perfect fit. You would never walk into a store and grab the first shoes you see without knowing your size and trying them on. So fess up if you are a mega size 12 or a petite size 5. And don't try to squeeze into the wrong size; it will lead only to pain and discomfort.

Are you sporting the perfect shoe size for your walk through life? You see, God custom fits us with the perfect combination of gifts and abilities for the walk He has planned for us in this life. By His grace, God lovingly designed your feet to be like no other. Your "shoe size"—your complete set of gifts and abilities—is uniquely yours.

Are you wearing the size God meant for you, or are you trying to force yourself into something else? For example, perhaps one woman takes on a demanding leadership role although her experience has taught her that she is better suited as a hard worker following another's lead. Maybe another woman accepts a detail-oriented role simply because the need is there, but she knows she can more easily see the big picture and details are not her area of strength. These women will struggle in their roles; they may even fail at them and frustrate other people in the process. They are simply wearing the wrong shoe size. Praise God that He can and *does* use our willing hearts and hands, yet sometimes we lack discernment about our God-given gifts and choose our commitments poorly. His mercy and grace in Christ covers us, forgiving us for the many times we have foolishly slipped into the wrong sizes and attempted to wear them.

Guided by the Holy Spirit, we glorify God and we serve others most effectively when we are aware of our shoe-size gifts and abilities and prayerfully consider how He wants to use them. We may recognize our gifts as those we have faithfully used in the past or those we have joyfully learned because of our eagerness and desire to serve in those ways. We may, instead, recognize our gifts when they jump out at us. We see the idea or need, and our hearts cry out, "That's my size! I can do that! I *want* to do that! That is my joy and my heart's delight!" What is your "shoe size"? Perhaps your gifts include giving, teaching, serving, listening, or supporting. (See Romans 12:6-8 for several important examples that are just a part of the many and varied gifts God gives His people.)

Recognizing and accepting your shoe size puts a bounce in your step and enables you to put your best foot forward in all He has called you to do. Don't be afraid to say, "I'm good at ____." Admitting your gifts is not boastful; it is God-pleasing when your gifts are credited to Him. Boast in your Creator, because "every good gift and every perfect gift is from above" (James 1:17). How and where will use your God-given gifts today?

> *Dear God, thank You for creating me with a unique shoe*
> *size set of gifts and abilities. Help me to find the perfect*
> *fit, that I may glorify You and serve others in Your Name.*
> *In Jesus' name I pray. Amen.*

Tickle the Toes!

Then our mouth was filled with laughter, and our tongue with shouts of joy. . . . "The LORD has done great things for us; we are glad." Psalm 126:2–3

Enormously pregnant with twins, I visited a popular brunch buffet with my husband and friends following church one Sunday. After a labored trip to the bathroom where I had painstakingly lined the seat with toilet paper, I waddled back toward the table, only to stop halfway and detour past the busy buffet line so I could peruse all the tasty fare. (I was eating for three, after all.) My protruding belly effectively blocked the view of my beautiful feet, and completely unaware that a long trail of toilet paper was stuck to my shoes, I trailed it all over the restaurant. Howling with laughter, my husband and friends repeatedly motioned to me to get my attention. Oblivious to the latest accessory attached to my feet, I happily waved back, which made them laugh all the harder. Quite spontaneously, I had "tickled the toes" of everyone at our table and several other patrons in the restaurant as well. I joined in their laughter later, after I realized what I had done.

Toes are one of the most ticklish parts of the body, and when we say that something tickles the toes, we mean that it makes us laugh joyfully! We are delighted and glad.

Are your toes easily tickled? Do you laugh joyfully and effortlessly, or do the worries and burdens of this life bog you down? (If you had spotted my shoes, decorated in toilet paper and modeled around the restaurant, would you have broken out in giggles, too, or would you have sat sullenly, distracted by your cares and troubles?)

The nation of Israel had faced many hardships and troubles. How long had they been without laughter? After years in captivity, Jerusalem was finally being restored! Only a remnant of God's people remained, but they were coming home. When the Lord brought back the captives, He tickled the toes of this joyful nation, who delighted themselves in Him, praising Him for their restoration! The psalmist proclaimed that their "mouth was filled with laughter." Shouts of joy rolled off their tongues! They could be glad at heart as they witnessed the great things the Lord had done for them, restoring their city and its fortunes.

Like Israel, you and I have faced (or will face) many troubles in this sinful life. We deal with adversity, pain, and hardship. In the midst of the most difficult times of loss and grief, we may think that nothing can possibly tickle our toes and make us laugh again. But God is faithful. He walks with us through our pain, restoring our joy. In the work of His Son, Jesus Christ, He frees us from our sins that have held us captive, and He brings us home to new life and salvation in Him. Filled with the Holy Spirit, we delight ourselves in the Lord, praising Him for our restoration!

O Lord, may You fill my mouth with laughter and my tongue with shouts of joy, for You have done great things for me in Christ! You have tickled my toes; I am glad. In Christ Jesus' name. Amen.

Two Left Feet

Such is the confidence that we have through Christ
toward God. Not that we are sufficient in ourselves
to claim anything as coming from us, but our sufficiency is from God, who has made us competent
to be ministers of a new covenant.
2 Corinthians 3:4–6

"Hey, Debbie, you wanna race?" Every time we got together to play, my roadrunner friend Todd wanted to race. I would shrug in reply, knowing the outcome would always be the same: his feet would leave mine in the dust. "I'll give you a head start again," he would coax (a predictable piece of persuasion). "This time, I'll even count to twenty!" That one worked on one particular occasion. I consented, thinking I might actually have a chance to win. We agreed on a finish line, and Todd called out, "Ready, set, GO!" I was off as fast as my chubby legs and my two left feet could carry me. Clumsily running with all my might, huffing and puffing, pumping my arms back and forth in awkward form, I was ahead! In the far distance behind me, I could hear Todd still counting. *Ha! He was eating my dust today!* Then came a blur of movement and a flash of light as he sped past me, securing his inevitable victory.

Running was fun and easy for him; God had blessed Todd and his siblings with springs for legs. But it was difficult and awkward for me. My pigeon-toed feet had been corrected years earlier, but I had no confidence in my ability to put one foot in front of the other successfully. I was sure I would trip and fall, come in last, and make a fool of myself. So I (and my two left feet) quit trying for many years.

Is there an area of your life where you feel you just don't measure up? Do you lack confidence in your ability to perform the task set before you? Clumsy and insecure, do you feel that all you can do is stumble along, making a fool of yourself? Have you quit trying? Perhaps the world has trained you to believe that you're incompetent because you don't measure up to its standards, or Satan has tried to trip you up, convincing you that your abilities are lacking and insufficient.

Know this: your sufficiency comes *not* from you, but from God in Christ! God has covered you in His perfect forgiveness and grace. He has empowered you with His Spirit, making you sufficient to complete exactly the task He has for you. And He has given you the task of being a minister of a new covenant in Christ, a covenant of grace and mercy. He has called you to minister in your vocation, in your home, in your church and community, and wherever else He may lead.

God will use your two left feet and He will be glorified through your efforts. When the watching world sees you giving your all as you share the Gospel, especially when they can tell it is difficult for you; when they know that you willingly serve, relying on God's strength and not your own; when they can tell that you walk (or run) with a confidence that is not your own—their lives will be touched. They will see the beautiful feet of Jesus in you.

Dear Lord, take my two left feet and make me competent
to be a minister of Your mercy and grace in Christ.
In Jesus' name. Amen.

Walk a Mile in Her Shoes

[Jesus said], "How can you say to your brother,
'Brother, let me take out the speck that is in your
eye,' when you yourself do not see the log that is
in your own eye? You hypocrite, first take the log
out of your own eye, and then you will see clearly
to take out the speck that is in your brother's eye."
Luke 6:42

Observing her, as I often did, I wondered how she could speak that way to the children. Didn't she have any patience or love for them? And why did she so often brag to other women about her many fine traits? Ooh, that really grated on my nerves. Didn't she know she was making a fool of herself? And her clothes. Oh, I could update her closet if she would just let me in it. Why wouldn't she take cues from me? I had subtly hinted several times that I could fix all of her issues, offering unsolicited advice. In so many words, I was saying, "If I were in your shoes, I would . . . " (You can imagine all the changes I had in mind for her that would improve her as a person.)

Then I learned more about her. After spending many hours together, meeting her family and learning about her past, I saw her in a different light. And I was ashamed of my previous attitude. How could I think that I had all the answers for someone whose walk was very different from mine? If it were possible for me to slip my feet into her shoes and walk a mile, perhaps I would not have been so judgmental.

That made me wonder how others see me. How do I speak to children? Do I appear to have patience and love as I interact with them? And how often do I turn conversations with other women to the topic of *me?* (Ouch. I know I often do.) My clothes don't appear in the latest fashion magazines. I'm not very good at receiving advice, either. When was the last time I paid attention to subtle cues someone was trying to give me? I have to admit that if another woman were in my shoes, she would probably behave differently.

How could I not have seen that a log was lodged in my eye? Sin had so blinded me to my own shortcomings that I foolishly focused on another's. My log needed to be removed before I could see clearly enough to help this woman take out the speck in hers. But I could not remove this log on my own. In love, God chose me in Christ, held me close, and loosened the log from my eye, forgiving my sins and giving me a repentant, changed heart. Filling me with His Spirit, He empowered me to see clearly, this time in love toward this woman. Walking a mile together, I in her shoes and she in mine, we could learn a lot from each other.

Perhaps you have had a similar experience. Have you been quick to judge someone else, focusing on the speck in her eye while ignoring the log in your own? Have you considered walking in her shoes with your beautiful feet? Know that God has chosen you in Christ; He holds you close and removes that nasty log, forgiving your sins and filling you with the Holy Spirit, enabling you to see clearly in love toward others.

Father God, thank You for lovingly removing the log from my eye, forgiving me through Your Son's death and resurrection. Guided by Your Spirit, may I walk a mile in others' shoes, able to see clearly in love toward them. In Jesus' name. Amen.

❧ Walking by Faith—Going Home ❧

They desire a better country, that is, a heavenly
one. Therefore God is not ashamed to be called
their God, for He has prepared for them a city.
Hebrews 11:16

How many places have you called home? Perhaps only one or two, or perhaps, like me, you have had many. My home has taken the shape of a college dorm, a small apartment, a townhouse, a duplex, and each of the many houses my family and I have rented or owned across several states. My very first home, a farm house in western South Dakota, is still home to my parents. Maybe that is why we say that we are "going home" when my family visits them. Wherever you call home, isn't it comforting when you can say, "I'm going home"?

Abraham was called by God to *leave* his home and *go* to a place he did not know. Hebrews 11 speaks of the faith of Abraham and others who walked by faith on this earth, sure of what they hoped for and certain of what they did not see. Abraham obediently followed God to the Promised Land where he lived in tents like a stranger in a foreign country because, by faith, he "desire[d] a better country"—he looked forward to a permanent home, prepared and built by God. Abraham trusted that God's promises would be fulfilled, not in his lifetime, but for his descendents. As Abraham walked this earth, a temporary resident, he knew his walk by faith would one day lead him to go home to heaven, the place of permanence.

No matter how many homes you or I have lived in, each is special and filled with memories, but not one is permanent.

Sometimes we don't like it when God calls us to go to a new and unknown place to serve Him. Sometimes we balk, saying, "But *this* is my home. I don't want to leave!" We cling tightly to the familiarity and the creature comforts of our current residence. Newly transplanted, we cry, "I want to go home!" to the place we had to leave behind.

Praise God that He is with us in every home and He forgives us when we cling too tightly to these earthly homes. We are Abraham's descendents, adopted as God's chosen children in Christ and recipients of God's promised salvation in Him. He fills us with faith and the power of the Holy Spirit, enabling us to obediently follow Him to each new place He has for us. Know it will soon feel like "home," but remember, too, that this earth is not our home. We are but strangers in this world. We walk by faith, knowing that our true home is in heaven; we are certain that what we hope for will one day be ours. Jesus said, "In My Father's house are many rooms. If it were not so, would I have told you that I go to prepare a place for you?" (John 14:2). When a loved one is called home to be with the Lord and we mourn our loss, what comfort we receive, walking by faith with our beautiful feet, knowing that one day we, too, will be going home to our Father's house and into the arms of Jesus, who has prepared a place for us.

> *Dear God, wherever I walk on this earth, by the power of Your Holy Spirit, I walk by faith! Thank you for the gift of salvation that is mine in Christ. I'm going home!*
> *In Jesus' name. Amen.*

Weary Feet

And let us not grow weary of doing good, for in
due season we will reap, if we do not give up.
Galatians 6:9

The wounded soldiers kept pouring into the hospital. She
heard the cries of pain all around as she scrambled to help
as many as she could. Stationed at the hospital closest to the
war front, she saw countless casualties every day. The work
was endless: cleaning wounds, administering medications,
prepping and assisting with surgery, holding hands, and most
of all, praying with the patients and giving them comfort and
hope. By nightfall, she often wondered if her weary feet would
stand another day. When morning arrived, she could tell
that the Lord was once again giving her the strength that she
needed to continue working on her weary feet.

Perhaps our feet have never known this kind of weariness,
but we know what it feels like to have tired feet. One woman
has weary feet from holding down a laborious job to help
support her family. Another's feet are weary because she
walks from village to village in the mission field, trying to
care for the people's basic needs while learning their
language and sharing the Gospel with them. Another has
weary feet from standing all day, attempting to teach a
roomful of noisy children. More weary feet work together
strenuously to help with cleanup efforts in a community
ravaged by a natural disaster. Still more women walk with
weary feet as they provide constant care for aging parents or
children with disabilities. And weary feet can be found in
homes, as women plod through the daily rigors of feeding

their families, cleaning the house, running errands, doing laundry, and more.

What do all these weary feet have in common? They are the beautiful feet of women who are *doing good*. They are being the feet of Jesus, bringing healing and hope, providing care and instruction, giving love and help wherever it is needed.

Your beautiful feet grow weary, too, as you do good for everyone around you. In fact, your feet may be so weary that you are tempted to give up. Our sinful flesh says, "It's not worth it. Just give up. Quit. Take care of yourself." Praise God that He does not give up on us, but leads our weary feet to Christ's cross where our Savior gave up His life for us, that we would receive forgiveness and eternal life in His name! Not because of any good we have done, but only out of His great love for us.

We draw strength from the Holy Spirit at work in God's Word; there we are exhorted to "not grow weary of doing good." Our feet may ache and we long to rest, but we do not become weary or give up because the power of the Spirit works through us. We have His promise that "in due season"—in other words, when the time is ripe and according to His will—He will reap a harvest through us. He will be glorified through our work. He will bring people to faith through our witness to them, and He will strengthen other believers in their faith as we diligently share His Word and live our lives doing good for others and therefore bringing honor to Him.

Lord, forgive me when I have grown so weary of doing good that I have given up. By Your Holy Spirit, empower me to share Your Word and do good for everyone, that You may be glorified and reap a harvest through me. In the name of Jesus I pray. Amen.